THE SIMPLE WISDOM OF
POPE FRANCIS

HOLD ON TO HOPE

Libreria Editrice Vaticana

United States Conference of Catholic Bishops
Washington, DC

First printing, November 2013
Second printing, December 2013

ISBN: 978-1-60137-442-4

CONTENTS

INTRODUCTION

You have in your possession one of the volumes of *The Simple Wisdom of Pope Francis* series, the first compilation of Pope Francis's teachings.

Immediately after his election on March 13th 2013, the world turned their eyes to the new Successor of Peter to notice Pope Francis's simple ways, humbleness, and his love for the poor and the sick.

This collection captures the wisdom of Pope Francis during his general audiences, which are regularly held on Wednesdays when the pope is in Rome. The general audiences give pilgrims and visitors a chance to "see the pope" and receive the Papal Blessing, or Apostolic Blessing, from the successor of the Apostle Peter. General audiences with the pope are spoken mainly in Italian, but also in English, French, Spanish, or other languages depending on the groups visiting. They consist of short, scripturally-based teachings in which the pope instructs the faithful across the world.

A final note: Francis's teachings also embrace the Year of Faith, which was instituted by our previous pope, Benedict XVI. The Year of Faith was "a summons to an authentic and renewed conversion to the Lord, the one Savior of the world" and spanned from October 11, 2012, through November 24, 2013. Pope Francis also references the *Catechism of the Catholic Church*, which is an organized presentation of the essential teachings of the Catholic Church.

It is our prayer that the teachings of the Holy Father within this series will be a source of hope and help in embracing the grace of faith a little more each day.

HOLY WEEK, A TIME OF THE GRACE OF THE LORD

MARCH 27, 2013

ST. PETER'S SQUARE

Brothers and Sisters, good morning!

I am glad to welcome you to my first General Audience. With deep gratitude and reverence I take up the "witness" from the hands of Benedict XVI, my beloved Predecessor. After Easter we shall resume the Catecheses for the Year of Faith. Today I would like to reflect a little on Holy Week. We began this Week with Palm Sunday—the heart of the whole Liturgical Year—in which we accompany Jesus in his Passion, death and Resurrection.

But what does living Holy Week mean to us? What does following Jesus on his journey to Calvary on his way to the Cross and the Resurrection mean? In his earthly mission Jesus walked the roads of the Holy Land; he called twelve simple people to stay with him, to share his journey and to continue his mission. He chose them from among the people full of faith in God's promises.

....

God does not wait for us to go to him but it is he who moves toward us.

He spoke to all without distinction: the great and the lowly, the rich young man and the poor widow, the powerful and the weak; he brought God's mercy and forgiveness; he healed, he comforted, he understood; he gave hope; he brought to all the presence of God who cares for every man and every woman, just as a good father and a good mother care for each one of their children.

God does not wait for us to go to him but it is he who moves toward us, without calculation, without quantification. That is what God is like. He always takes the first step, he comes toward us.

Jesus lived the daily reality of the most ordinary people: he was moved as he faced the crowd that seemed like a flock without a shepherd; he wept before the sorrow that Martha and Mary felt at the death of their brother, Lazarus; he called a publican to be his disciple; he also suffered betrayal by a friend. In him God has given us the certitude that he is with us, he is among us. "Foxes," he, Jesus, said, "have holes, and birds of the air have nests, but the Son of man has nowhere to lay his head" (Mt 8:20). Jesus has no house, because his house is the people, it is we who are his dwelling place, his mission is to open God's doors to all, to be the presence of God's love.

In Holy Week we live the crowning moment of this journey, of this plan of love that runs through the entire history of the relations between God and humanity. Jesus enters Jerusalem to take his last step with which he sums up the whole of his existence. He gives himself without reserve, he keeps nothing for himself, not even life. At the Last Supper, with his friends, he breaks the bread and passes the cup round "for us." The Son of God offers himself to us, he puts his Body and his Blood into our hands, so as to be with us always, to dwell among us. And in the Garden of Olives, and likewise in the trial before Pilate, he puts up no resistance, he gives himself; he is the suffering Servant, foretold by Isaiah, who empties himself, even unto death (cf. Is 53:12).

Jesus does not experience this love that leads to his sacrifice passively or as a fatal destiny. He does not of course conceal his deep human distress as he faces a violent death, but with absolute trust commends himself to the Father. Jesus gave himself up to death voluntarily in order to reciprocate the love of God the Father, in perfect union with his will, to demonstrate his love for us. On the Cross Jesus "loved me and gave himself for me" (Gal 2:20). Each one of us can say: "He loved me and gave himself for me." Each one can say this "for me."

What is the meaning of all this for us? It means that this is my, your and our road too. Living Holy Week, following Jesus not only with the emotion of the heart; living Holy Week, following Jesus means learning to come out of ourselves—as I said last Sunday—in order to go to meet others, to go toward the outskirts of existence, to be the first to take a step toward our brothers and our sisters, especially those who are the most distant, those who are forgotten, those who are most in need of understanding, comfort and help. There is such a great need to bring the living presence of Jesus, merciful and full of love!

Living Holy Week means entering ever more deeply into the logic of God, into the logic of the Cross, which is not primarily that of suffering and death, but rather that of love and of the gift of self which brings life. It means entering into the logic of the Gospel. Following and accompanying Christ, staying with him, demands "coming out of ourselves," requires us to be outgoing; to come out of ourselves, out of a dreary way of living faith that has become a habit, out of the temptation to withdraw into our own plans which end by shutting out God's creative action.

God came out of himself to come among us, he pitched his tent among us to bring to us his mercy that saves and gives hope. Nor must we be satisfied with staying in the pen of the ninety-nine sheep if we want to follow him

4

and to remain with him; we too must "go out" with him to seek the lost sheep, the one that has strayed the furthest. Be sure to remember: coming out of ourselves, just as Jesus, just as God came out of himself in Jesus and Jesus came out of himself for all of us.

Someone might say to me: "But Father, I don't have time," "I have so many things to do," "It's difficult," "What can I do with my feebleness and my sins, with so many things?" We are often satisfied with a few prayers, with a distracted and sporadic participation in Sunday Mass, with a few charitable acts; but we do not have the courage "to come out" to bring Christ to others. We are a bit like St. Peter. As soon as Jesus speaks of his Passion, death and Resurrection, of the gift of himself, of love for all, the Apostle takes him aside and reproaches him. What Jesus says upsets his plans, seems unacceptable, threatens the security he had built for himself, his idea of the Messiah. And Jesus looks at his disciples and addresses to Peter what may possibly be the harshest words in the Gospels: "Get behind me Satan! For you are not on the side of God, but of men" (Mk 8:33). God always thinks with mercy: do not forget this. God always thinks mercifully. He is the merciful Father! God thinks like the father waiting for the son and goes to meet him, he spots him coming when he is still far off . . .

What does this mean? That he went every day to see if his son was coming home: this is our merciful Father. It indicates that he was waiting for him with longing on the terrace of his house. God thinks like the Samaritan who did not pass by the unfortunate man, pitying him or looking at him from the other side of the road, but helped him without asking for anything in return; without asking whether he was a Jew, a pagan or a Samaritan, whether he was rich or poor: he asked for nothing. He went to help him: God is like this. God thinks like the shepherd who lays down his life in order to defend and save his sheep.

Holy Week is a time of grace which the Lord gives us *to open the doors* of our heart, of our life, of our parishes—what a pity so many parishes are closed!—of the movements, of the associations; and "to come out" in order to meet others, to make ourselves close, to bring them the light and joy of our faith. To come out always! And to do so with God's love and tenderness, with respect and with patience, knowing that God takes our hands, our feet, our heart, and guides them and makes all our actions fruitful.

I hope that we all will live these days well, following the Lord courageously, carrying within us a ray of his love for all those we meet.

INSTRUMENTS OF CHRIST'S GRACE

Easter Monday • April 1, 2013

St. Peter's Square

Dear Brothers and Sisters,

Good Morning and a Happy Easter to you all! I thank you for coming here today too in such large numbers, to share in the joy of Easter, the central mystery of our faith. May the power of Christ's Resurrection reach every person—especially those who are suffering—and all the situations most in need of trust and hope.

Christ has fully triumphed over evil once and for all, but it is up to us, to the people of every epoch, to welcome this victory into our life and into the actual situations of history and society. For this reason it seems to me important to emphasize what we ask God today in the liturgy. "O God, who give constant increase / to your Church by new offspring, / grant that your servants may hold fast in their lives / to the Sacrament they have received in faith" (Collect, Monday within the Octave of Easter).

It is true, yes, Baptism that makes us children of God and the Eucharist that unites us to Christ must become life, that is, they must be expressed in attitudes, behavior, gestures and decisions. The grace contained in the Sacraments of Easter is an enormous potential for the renewal

....

Everything passes through the human heart.

of our personal existence, of family life, of social relations. However everything passes through the human heart: if I let myself be touched by the grace of the Risen Christ, if I let him change me in that aspect of mine which is not good, which can hurt me and others, I allow the victory of Christ to be affirmed in my life, to broaden its beneficial action. This is the power of grace! Without grace we can do nothing. Without grace we can do nothing! And with the grace of Baptism and of Eucharistic Communion I can become an instrument of God's mercy, of that beautiful mercy of God.

To express in life the sacrament we have received: dear brothers and sisters, this is our daily duty, but I would also say our daily joy! The joy of feeling we are instruments of Christ's grace, like branches of the vine that is Christ himself, brought to life by the sap of his Spirit!

Let us pray together, in the name of the dead and Risen Lord and through the intercession of Mary Most Holy, that the Paschal Mystery may work profoundly within us and in our time so that hatred may give way to love, falsehood to truth, revenge to forgiveness, and sadness to joy.

WOMEN, THE FIRST WITNESSES OF THE RESURRECTION

APRIL 3, 2013

ST. PETER'S SQUARE

Dear Brothers and Sisters, good morning,

Today let us take up the Catecheses of the Year of Faith. In the *Creed* we repeat these words: "and rose again on the third day in accordance with the Scriptures." This is the very event that we are celebrating: the Resurrection of Jesus, the center of the Christian message which has echoed from the beginning and was passed on so that it would come down to us. St. Paul wrote to the Christians of Corinth: "I delivered to you as of first importance what I also received, that Christ died for our sins in accordance with the scriptures, that he was buried, that he was raised on the third day in accordance with the scriptures and that he appeared to Cephas, then to the Twelve" (1 Cor 15:3-5). This brief profession of faith proclaims the Paschal Mystery itself with the first appearances of the Risen One to Peter and the Twelve: *the death and Resurrection of Jesus are the very heart of our hope.*

Without this faith in the death and Resurrection of Jesus our hope would be weak; but it would not even be hope; or precisely the death and Resurrection of Jesus are the heart of our hope. The Apostle said: "If Christ has not been raised, your faith is futile and you are still in your sins" (v. 17). Unfortunately, efforts have often been made to blur faith in the Resurrection of Jesus and doubts have crept in,

....

Do not view life as solely horizontal.

even among believers. It is a little like that "rosewater" faith, as we say; it is not a strong faith. And this is due to superficiality and sometimes to indifference, busy as we are with a thousand things considered more important than faith, or because we have a view of life that is solely horizontal. However, it is the Resurrection itself that opens us to greater hope, for it opens our life and the life of the world to the eternal future of God, to full happiness, to the certainty that evil, sin and death may be overcome. And this leads to living daily situations with greater trust, to facing them with courage and determination. Christ's Resurrection illuminates these everyday situations with a new light. The Resurrection of Christ is our strength!

But how was the truth of faith in Christ's Resurrection passed down to us? There are two kinds of testimony in the New Testament: some are in the form of a profession of faith, that is, of concise formulas that indicate the center of faith; while others are in the form of an account of the event of the Resurrection and of the facts connected with it.

The former, in the form of a profession of faith, for example, is the one we have just heard, or that of the Letter to the Romans in which St. Paul wrote: "If you confess with your lips that 'Jesus is Lord!' and believe in your heart that God raised him from the dead, you will be saved" (10:9). From the Church's very first steps faith in the Mystery of the death and Resurrection of Christ is firm and clear. Today, however, I would like to reflect on the latter, on the testimonies in the form of a narrative which we find in the Gospels. First of all let us note that the first witnesses of this event were the women. At dawn they went to the tomb to anoint Jesus' body and found the first sign: the empty tomb (cf. Mk 16:1). Their meeting with a messenger of God followed. He announced: "Jesus of Nazareth, the Crucified One, has risen, he is not here" (cf. vv. 5-6). The women were motivated by love and were able to accept this announcement with faith:

they believed and passed it on straightaway, they did not keep it to themselves but passed it on.

They could not contain their joy in knowing that Jesus was alive, or the hope that filled their hearts. This should happen in our lives too. Let us feel the joy of being Christian! We believe in the Risen One who conquered evil and death! Let us have the courage to "come out of ourselves" to take this joy and this light to all the places of our life! The Resurrection of Christ is our greatest certainty; he is our most precious treasure! How can we not share this treasure, this certainty with others? It is not only for us, it is to be passed on, to be shared with others. Our testimony is precisely this.

Another point: in the profession of faith in the New Testament only men are recorded as witnesses of the Resurrection, the Apostles, but not the women. This is because, according to the Judaic Law of that time, women and children could not bear a trustworthy, credible witness. Instead in the Gospels women play a fundamental lead role. Here we can grasp an element in favor of the historicity of the Resurrection: if it was an invented event, in the context of that time it would not have been linked with the evidence of women. Instead the Evangelists simply recounted what happened: women were the first witnesses. This implies that God does not choose in accordance with human criteria: the first witnesses of the birth of Jesus were shepherds, simple, humble people; the first witnesses of the Resurrection were women. And this is beautiful. This is part of the mission of women; of mothers, of women! Witnessing to their children, to their grandchildren, that Jesus is alive, is living, is risen. Mothers and women, carry on witnessing to this! It is the heart that counts for God, how open to him we are, whether we are like trusting children.

However this also makes us think about how women, in the Church and on the journey of faith, had and still have today a special role in opening the doors to the Lord, in following him and in communicating his Face, for the gaze of faith is always in need of the simple and profound gaze of love.

> **Faith is professed with the lips and with the heart, with words and with love.**

The Apostles and disciples find it harder to believe. The women, not so. Peter runs to the tomb but stops at the empty tomb; Thomas has to touch the wounds on Jesus' body with his hands. On our way of faith it is also important to know and to feel that God loves us and not to be afraid to love him. Faith is professed with the lips and with the heart, with words and with love.

After his appearances to the women, others follow. Jesus makes himself present in a new way, he is the Crucified One but his body is glorified; he did not return to earthly life but returned in a new condition. At first they do not recognize him and it is only through his words and gestures that their eyes are opened. The meeting with the Risen One transforms, it gives faith fresh strength and a steadfast foundation. For us too there are many signs through which the Risen One makes himself known: Sacred Scripture, the Eucharist, the other Sacraments, charity, all those acts of love which bring a ray of the Risen One. Let us permit ourselves to be illuminated by Christ's Resurrection, let him transform us with his power, so that through us too the signs of death may give way to signs of life in the world.

I see that there are large numbers of young people in the square. There you are! I say to you: carry this certainty ahead: the Lord is alive and walks beside you through life. This is your mission! Carry this hope onward. May you be anchored to this hope: this anchor which is in heaven; hold the rope firmly, be anchored and carry hope forward. You, witnesses of Jesus, pass on the witness that Jesus is alive and this will give us hope, it will give hope to this world, which has aged somewhat, because of wars, because of evil and because of sin. Press on, young people!

CHRIST, MERCY INCARNATE

SECOND SUNDAY OF EASTER

DIVINE MERCY SUNDAY • APRIL 7, 2013

ST. PETER'S SQUARE

Dear Brothers and Sisters, good morning!

On this Sunday which brings the Octave of Easter to a close I renew to everyone my good wishes for Easter in the very words of the Risen Jesus: "*Peace be with you*" (Jn 20:19, 21, 26). This is not a greeting nor even a simple good wish: it is a gift, indeed, *the* precious gift that Christ offered his disciples after he had passed through death and hell.

He gives peace, as he had promised: "Peace I leave with you; my peace I give to you; not as the world gives do I give to you" (Jn 14:27). This peace is the fruit of the victory of God's love over evil, it is the fruit of forgiveness. And it really is like this: true peace, that profound peace, comes from experiencing God's mercy. Today is Divine Mercy Sunday, as John Paul II—who closed his eyes to the world on the eve of this very day—wanted it to be.

John's Gospel tells us that Jesus appeared twice to the Apostles enclosed in the Upper Room: the first time on the evening of the Resurrection itself and on that occasion Thomas, who said unless I see and touch I will not believe, was absent. The second time, eight days later, Thomas was there as well. And Jesus said, speaking directly to him, I invite you to look at my wounds, to touch them; then Thomas exclaimed: "My Lord and my God!" (Jn 20:28). So Jesus said: "Have you believed because you have seen me? Blessed are those who have not seen and yet believe" (v. 29); and who were those who believed without seeing? Other disciples, other men and women

....

True peace comes from experiencing God's mercy.

of Jerusalem, who, on the testimony of the Apostles and the women, believed, even though they had not met the Risen Jesus. This is a very important word about faith, we can call it *the beatitude of faith*. Blessed are those who have not seen but have believed: this is the beatitude of faith! In every epoch and in every place blessed are those who, on the strength of the word of God proclaimed in the Church and witnessed by Christians, believe that Jesus Christ is the love of God incarnate, Mercy incarnate. And this applies for each one of us!

As well as his peace, Jesus gave the Apostles the Holy Spirit so that they could spread the forgiveness of sins in the world, that forgiveness which only God can give and which came at the price of the Blood of the Son (cf. Jn 20:21-23). The Church is sent by the Risen Christ to pass on to men and women the forgiveness of sins and thereby make the Kingdom of love grow, to sow peace in hearts so that they may also be strengthened in relationships, in every society, in institutions.

....

He has pardoned us with his Blood and pardons us every time we go to him to ask his forgiveness.

And the Spirit of the Risen Christ drove out fear from the Apostles' hearts and impelled them to leave the Upper Room in order to spread the Gospel. Let us too have greater courage in witnessing to our faith in the Risen Christ! We must not be afraid of being Christian and living as Christians! We must have this courage to go and proclaim the Risen Christ, for he is our peace, he made peace with his love, with his forgiveness, with his Blood, and with his mercy.

Dear friends, this afternoon I shall celebrate the Eucharist in the Basilica of St. John Lateran, which is the Cathedral of the Bishop of Rome. Together let us pray the Virgin Mary that she help us, Bishop and People, to walk in faith and charity, ever trusting in the Lord's mercy: he always awaits us, loves us, has pardoned us with his Blood and pardons us every time we go to him to ask his forgiveness. Let us trust in his mercy!

THE RISEN CHRIST, THE HOPE THAT NEVER DISAPPOINTS

April 10, 2013

St. Peter's Square

Dear Brothers and Sisters, good morning!

In our previous Catechesis, we reflected on the event of the Resurrection of Jesus, in which the women played a special role. Today I would like to reflect on its saving capacity. What does the Resurrection mean for our life? And why is our faith in vain without it?

Our faith is founded on Christ's death and Resurrection, just as a house stands on its foundations: if they give way, the whole house collapses. Jesus gave himself on the Cross, taking the burden of our sins upon himself and descending into the abyss of death, then in the Resurrection he triumphed over them, took them away and opened before us the path to rebirth and to a new life.

St. Peter summed this up at the beginning of his First Letter, as we heard: "Blessed be the God and Father of our Lord Jesus Christ! By his great mercy we have been born anew to a living hope through the Resurrection of Jesus Christ from the dead, and to an inheritance which is imperishable, undefiled, and unfading" (1:3-4).

The Apostle tells us that with the Resurrection of Jesus something absolutely new happens: we are set free from the slavery of sin and become children of God; that is, we are born to new life. When is this accomplished for us? In the sacrament of Baptism. In ancient times, it was customarily received through immersion. The person who was to be baptized walked down into the great basin of the Baptistery, stepping out of his clothes, and the Bishop or Priest poured water on his head three times, baptizing him in the name of the Father, of the Son, and of the Holy Spirit. Then the baptized person emerged from the basin and put on a new robe, the white one; in other words, by immersing himself in the death and Resurrection of Christ he was born to new life. He had become a son of God. In his Letter to the Romans St. Paul wrote: "You have received the spirit of sonship. When we cry 'Abba! Father!' it is the Spirit himself bearing witness with our spirit that we are children of God" (Rom 8:15-16).

It is the Spirit himself whom we received in Baptism who teaches us, who spurs us to say to God: "Father," or, rather, "Abba!," which means "papa" or ["dad"]. Our God is like this: he is a dad to us. The Holy Spirit creates within us this new condition as children of God. And this is the greatest gift we have received from the Paschal Mystery of Jesus. Moreover God treats us as children, he understands us, he forgives us, he embraces us, he loves us even when we err. In the Old Testament, the Prophet Isaiah was already affirming that even if a mother could forget her child, God never forgets us at any moment (cf. 49:15). And this is beautiful!

Yet this filial relationship with God is not like a treasure that we keep in a corner of our life but must be increased. It must be nourished every day with listening to the word of God, with prayer, with participation in the sacraments, especially Reconciliation and the Eucharist, and with love. We can live as children! And this is our dignity—we have the dignity of children. We should behave as true children! This means that every day we must let Christ transform us and conform us to him; it means striving to live as Christians, endeavoring to follow him in spite of seeing our limitations and weaknesses. The temptation to set God aside in order to put ourselves at the center is always at the door, and the experience of sin injures our Christian life, our being children of God. For this reason we must have the courage of faith not to allow ourselves to be guided by the mentality that tells us: "God is not necessary, he is not important for you," and so forth. It is exactly the opposite: only by behaving as children of God, without despairing at our shortcomings, at our sins, only by feeling loved by him will our life be new, enlivened by serenity and joy. God is our strength! God is our hope!

Dear brothers and sisters, we must be the first to have this steadfast hope and we must be a visible, clear and radiant sign of it for everyone. The Risen Lord is the hope that never fails, that never disappoints (cf. Rom 5:5). Hope does not let us down—the hope of the Lord! How often in our life do hopes vanish, how often do the expectations we have in our

We must be a visible, clear, and radiant sign of hope for everyone.

heart come to nothing! Our hope as Christians is strong, safe and sound on this earth, where God has called us to walk, and it is open to eternity because it is founded on God who is always faithful. We must not forget: God is always faithful to us. Being raised with Christ through Baptism, with the gift of faith, an inheritance that is incorruptible, prompts us to seek God's things more often, to think of him more often and to pray to him more.

Being Christian is not just obeying orders but means being in Christ, thinking like him, acting like him, loving like him; it means letting him take possession of our life and change it, transform it and free it from the darkness of evil and sin.

Dear brothers and sisters, let us point out the Risen Christ to those who ask us to account for the hope that is in us (cf. 1 Pt 3:15). Let us point him out with the proclamation of the word, but above all with our lives as people who have been raised. Let us show the joy of being children of God, the freedom that living in Christ gives us which is true freedom, the freedom that saves us from the slavery of evil, of sin and of death! Looking at the heavenly homeland, we shall receive new light and fresh strength, both in our commitment and in our daily efforts.

This is a precious service that we must give to this world of ours which all too often no longer succeeds in raising its gaze on high, no longer succeeds in raising its gaze to God.

WE FEEL THE LIVING AND COMFORTING PRESENCE OF THE RISEN JESUS

THIRD SUNDAY OF EASTER • APRIL 14, 2013

ST. PETER'S SQUARE

Dear Brothers and Sisters, good morning!

I would like to reflect briefly on the passage from the Acts of the Apostles that is read in the Liturgy of this Third Sunday of Easter. This text says that the Apostles' first preaching in Jerusalem filled the city with the news that Jesus was truly risen in accordance with the Scriptures and was the Messiah foretold by the Prophets. The chief priests and elders of the city were endeavoring to crush the nascent community of believers in Christ and had the Apostles thrown into jail, ordering them to stop teaching in his name. But Peter and the other Eleven answered: "We must obey God rather than men. The God of our fathers raised Jesus . . . exalted him at his right hand as Leader and Savior . . . And we are witnesses to these things, and so is the Holy Spirit whom God has given to those who obey him" (Acts 5:29-32). They therefore had the Apostles scourged and once again ordered them to stop speaking in the name of Jesus. And they went away, as Scripture says, "rejoicing that they were counted worthy to suffer dishonor for the name" of Jesus (v. 41).

I ask myself: where did the first disciples find the strength to bear this witness? And that is not all: what was the source of their joy and of their courage to preach despite the obstacles and violence? Let us not forget that the Apostles were simple people; they were neither scribes nor doctors of the law, nor did they belong to the class of priests. With their limitations and with the authorities against them how did they manage to fill Jerusalem with their teaching (cf. Acts 5:28)?

It is clear that only the presence with them of the Risen Lord and the action of the Holy Spirit can explain this fact. The Lord who was with them and the Spirit who was impelling them to preach explain this extraordinary fact. Their faith was based on such a strong personal experience of the dead and Risen Christ that they feared nothing and no one, and even saw persecution as a cause of honor that enabled them to follow in Jesus' footsteps and to be like him, witnessing with their life.

This history of the first Christian community tells us something very important which applies to the Church in all times and also to us. When a person truly knows Jesus Christ and believes in him, that person experiences his presence in life as well as the power of his Resurrection and cannot but communicate this experience. And if this person meets with

Behave like Jesus. Always answer with love and with the power of truth.

misunderstanding or adversity, he behaves like Jesus in his Passion: he answers with love and with the power of the truth.

In praying the *Regina Caeli* together, let us ask for the help of Mary Most Holy so that the Church throughout the world may proclaim the Resurrection of the Lord with candor and courage and give credible witness to it with signs of brotherly love. Brotherly love is the closest testimony we can give that Jesus is alive with us, that Jesus is risen.

Let us pray in a special way for Christians who are suffering persecution; in our day there are so many Christians who are suffering persecution—so, so many, in a great many countries: let us pray for them, with love, from our heart. May they feel the living and comforting presence of the Risen Lord.

HE ASCENDED INTO HEAVEN AND IS SEATED AT THE RIGHT HAND OF THE FATHER

APRIL 17, 2013

ST. PETER'S SQUARE

Dear Brothers and Sisters, good morning!

In the Creed we say that Jesus "ascended into heaven and is seated at the right hand of the Father." Jesus' earthly life culminated with the Ascension, when he passed from this world to the Father and was raised to sit on his right. What does this event mean? How does it affect our life? What does contemplating Jesus seated at the right hand of the Father mean? Let us permit the Evangelist Luke to guide us in this.

Let us start from the moment when Jesus decided to make his last pilgrimage to Jerusalem. St. Luke notes: "When the days drew near for him to be received up, he set his face to go to Jerusalem" (Lk 9:51). While he was "going up" to the Holy City, where his own "exodus" from this life was to occur, Jesus already saw the destination, heaven, but he knew well that the way which would lead him to the glory of the Father passed through the Cross, through obedience to the divine design of love for mankind. The *Catechism of the Catholic Church* states that "the lifting up of Jesus on the cross signifies and announces his lifting up by his Ascension into heaven" (no. 662).

We too should be clear in our Christian life that entering the glory of God demands daily fidelity to his will, even when it demands sacrifice and sometimes requires us to change our plans. The Ascension of Jesus actually happened on the Mount of Olives, close to the place where he had withdrawn to pray before the Passion in order to remain in deep union with the Father: once again we see that prayer gives us the grace to be faithful to God's plan.

At the end of his Gospel, St. Luke gives a very concise account of the event of the Ascension. Jesus led his disciples "out as far as Bethany, and lifting up his hands he blessed them. While he blessed them, he parted from them, and was carried up into heaven. And they worshipped him, and returned to Jerusalem with great joy, and were continually in the temple blessing God" (Lk 24:50-53). This is what St. Luke says.

I would like to note two elements in the account. First of all, during the Ascension Jesus made the priestly gesture of blessing, and the disciples certainly expressed their faith with prostration, they knelt with bowed heads; this is a first important point: Jesus is the one eternal High Priest who with his Passion passed through death and the tomb and ascended into heaven. He is with God the Father where he intercedes for ever in our favor (cf. Heb 9:24). As St. John says in his First Letter, he is our Advocate: How beautiful it is to hear this! When someone is summoned by the judge or is involved in legal proceedings, the first thing he does is to seek a lawyer to defend him. We have One who always defends us, who defends us from the snares of devil, who defends us from ourselves and from our sins!

Dear brothers and sisters, we have this Advocate; let us not be afraid to turn to him to ask forgiveness, to ask for a blessing, to ask for mercy! He always pardons us, he is our Advocate: he always defends us! Don't forget this! The Ascension of Jesus into heaven acquaints us with this deeply consoling reality on our journey: in Christ, true God and true man, our humanity was taken to God. Christ opened the path to us. He is like a roped guide climbing a mountain who, on reaching the summit, pulls us up to him and leads us to God. If we entrust our life to him, if we let ourselves be guided by him, we are certain to be in safe hands, in the hands of our Savior, of our Advocate.

A second element: St. Luke says that having seen Jesus ascending into heaven, the Apostles returned to Jerusalem "with great joy." This seems to us a little odd. When we are separated from our relatives, from our friends, because of a definitive departure and, especially, death, there is usually a natural sadness in us since we will no longer see their face, no longer hear their voice, or enjoy their love, their presence. The Evangelist instead emphasizes the profound joy of the Apostles.

....

Jesus is like a guide climbing a mountain who pulls us up to him and leads us to God.

But how could this be? Precisely because, with the gaze of faith they understand that although he has been removed from their sight, Jesus stays with them for ever, he does not abandon them and in the glory of the Father supports them, guides them and intercedes for them.

St. Luke too recounts the event of the Ascension—at the beginning of the Acts of the Apostles—to emphasize that this event is like the link of the chain that connects Jesus' earthly life to the life of the Church. Here St. Luke also speaks of the cloud that hid Jesus from the sight of the disciples, who stood gazing at him ascending to God (cf. Acts 1:9-10). Then two men in white robes appeared and asked them not to stand there looking up to heaven but to nourish their lives and their witness with the certainty that Jesus will come again in the same way in which they saw him ascending into heaven (cf. Acts 1:10-11). This is the invitation to base our contemplation on Christ's lordship, to find in him the strength to spread the Gospel and to witness to it in everyday life: contemplation and action, *ora et labora*, as St. Benedict taught, are both necessary in our life as Christians.

Dear brothers and sisters, the Ascension does not point to Jesus' absence, but tells us that he is alive in our midst in a new way. He is no longer in a specific place in the world as he was before the Ascension. He is now in the lordship of God, present in every space and time, close to each one of us. In our life we are never alone: we have this Advocate who awaits us, who defends us. We are never alone: the Crucified and Risen Lord guides us. We have with us a multitude of brothers and sisters who, in silence and concealment, in their family life and at work, in their problems and hardships, in their joys and hopes, live faith daily and together with us bring the world the lordship of God's love, in the Risen Jesus Christ, ascended into Heaven, our own Advocate who pleads for us. Many thanks.

I AND THE FATHER
ARE ONE

Fourth Sunday of Easter • April 21, 2013

St. Peter's Square

Dear Brothers and Sisters, good morning!

The Fourth Sunday of the Season of Easter is characterized by the Gospel of the Good Shepherd—in Chapter 10 of St. John—which is read every year. Today's passage records these words of Jesus: "My sheep hear my voice, and I know them, and they follow me; and I give them eternal life, and they shall never perish, and no one shall snatch them out of my hand. My Father, who has given them to me is greater than all, and no one is able to snatch them out of the Father's hand. I and the Father are one" (10:27-30). These four verses contain the whole of Jesus' message; it is the nucleus of his Gospel: he calls us to share in his relationship with the Father, and this is eternal life.

Jesus wants to establish with his friends a relationship which mirrors his own relationship with the Father: a relationship of reciprocal belonging in full trust, in intimate communion. To express this profound understanding, this relationship of friendship, Jesus uses the image of the shepherd with his sheep: he calls them and they recognize his voice, they respond to his call and follow him. This parable is very beautiful! The mystery of his voice is evocative: only think that from our mother's womb we learn to recognize her voice and that of our father; it is from the tone of a voice that we perceive love or contempt, affection or coldness. Jesus' voice is unique! If we learn to distinguish it, he guides us on the path of life, a path that goes beyond even the abyss of death.

Hear the voice of the Lord in your desires and your worries.

However Jesus, at a certain point, said: "my Father, who has given them to me . . . " (Jn 10:29), referring to his sheep. This is very important, it is a profound mystery, far from easy to understand. If I feel drawn to Jesus, if his voice warms my heart, it is thanks to God the Father who has sown within me the desire for love, for truth, for life, for beauty . . . and Jesus is all this in fullness! This helps us understand the mystery of vocation and especially of the call to a special consecration. Sometimes Jesus calls

34

us, he invites us to follow him, but perhaps we do not realize that it is he who is calling, like what happened to the young Samuel. There are many young people today, here in the Square. There are large numbers of you, aren't there? It's clear . . . Look! Here in the Square today there are so many of you! I would like to ask you: have you sometimes heard the Lord's voice, in a desire, in a worry, did he invite you to follow him more closely? Have you heard him? I can't hear you? There! Have you wanted to be apostles of Jesus? We must bet on youth for the great ideals. Do you think this? Do you agree? Ask Jesus what he wants of you and be brave! Be brave! Ask him this!

Behind and before every vocation to the priesthood or to the consecrated life there is always the strong and intense prayer of someone: a grandmother, a grandfather, a mother, a father, a community . . . This is why Jesus said: "Pray therefore the Lord of the harvest," that is, God the Father, "to send out laborers into his harvest" (Mt 9:38). Vocations are born in prayer and from prayer; and only through prayer can they persevere and bear fruit. I am pleased to stress this today, which is the "World Day of Prayer for Vocations."

Let us pray in particular for the new Priests of the Diocese of Rome whom I have had the joy to ordain this morning. And let us invoke the intercession of Mary. Today there were ten young men who said "yes" to Jesus and they have been ordained priests this morning. This is beautiful!

Let us invoke the intercession of Mary who is the Woman of the "yes." Mary said "yes" throughout her life! She learned to recognize Jesus' voice from the time when she carried him in her womb. May Mary, our Mother, help us to know Jesus' voice better and better and to follow it, so as to walk on the path of life! Thank you.

Thank you so much for your greeting, but greet Jesus too. Shout "Jesus" very loudly . . . Let us all pray together to Our Lady.

THE END OF TIME

April 24, 2013

St. Peter's Square

Dear Brothers and Sisters, good morning!

In the Creed we profess that Jesus "will come again in glory to judge the living and the dead." Human history begins with the creation of man and woman in God's likeness and ends with the Last Judgment of Christ. These two poles of history are often forgotten; and, at times, especially faith in Christ's return and in the Last Judgment, are not so clear and firm in Christian hearts. In his public life Jesus frequently reflected on the reality of his Final Coming. Today I would like to reflect on three Gospel texts that help us to penetrate this mystery: those of the ten virgins, of the talents and of the Last Judgment. All three are part of Jesus' discourse on the end of time which can be found in the Gospel of St. Matthew.

Let us remember first of all that in the Ascension the Son of God brought to the Father our humanity, which he had taken on, and that he wants to draw all to himself, to call the whole world to be welcomed in God's embrace so that at the end of history the whole of reality may be consigned to the Father. Yet there is this "immediate time" between the First and the Final Coming of Christ, and that is the very time in which we are living.

·····································

Get ready for an encounter, a beautiful encounter.

The parable of the ten virgins fits into this context of "immediate" time (cf. Mt 25:1-13). They are ten maidens who are awaiting the arrival of the Bridegroom, but he is late and they fall asleep. At the sudden announcement that the Bridegroom is arriving they prepare to welcome him, but while five of them, who are wise, have oil to burn in their lamps, the others, who are foolish, are left with lamps that have gone out because they have no oil for them. While they go to get some oil the Bridegroom arrives and the foolish virgins find that the door to the hall of the marriage feast is shut.

They knock on it again and again, but it is now too late, the Bridegroom answers: I do not know you. The Bridegroom is the Lord, and the time of waiting for his arrival is the time he gives to us, to all of us, before his Final Coming with mercy and patience; it is a time of watchfulness; a time in which we must keep alight the lamps of faith, hope and charity, a time in which to keep our heart open to goodness, beauty and truth. It is a time to live in accordance with God, because we do not know either the day or the hour of Christ's return. What he asks of us is to be ready for the encounter—ready for an encounter, for a beautiful encounter, the encounter with Jesus, which means being able to see the signs of his presence, keeping our faith alive with prayer, with the sacraments, and taking care not to fall asleep so as to not forget about God. The life of slumbering Christians is a sad life, it is not a happy life. Christians must be happy, with the joy of Jesus. Let us not fall asleep!

The second parable, the parable of the talents, makes us think about the relationship between how we use the gifts we have received from God and his return, when he will ask us what use we made of them (cf. Mt 25:14-30). We are well acquainted with the parable: before his departure the master gives a few talents to each of his servants to ensure that they will be put to good use during his absence. He gives five to the first servant, two to the second one and one to the third. In the period of their master's absence, the first two servants increase their talents—these are ancient coins—whereas the third servant prefers to bury his and to return it to his master as it was.

On his return, the master judges what they have done: he praises the first two while he throws the third one out into the outer darkness because, through fear, he had hidden his talent, withdrawing into himself. A Christian who withdraws into himself, who hides everything that the Lord has given him, is a Christian who . . . he is not a Christian! He is a Christian who does not thank God for everything God has given him!

This tells us that the expectation of the Lord's return is the time of action—we are in the time of action— the time in which we should bring God's gifts to fruition, not for ourselves but for him, for the Church, for others. The time to seek to increase goodness in the world always; and in particular, in this period of crisis, today, it is important not to turn in on ourselves, burying our own talent, our spiritual, intellectual, and material riches, everything that the Lord has given us, but, rather to open ourselves, to be supportive, to be attentive to others.

In the square I have seen that there are many young people here: it is true, isn't it? Are there many young people? Where are they? I ask you who are just setting out on your journey through life: have you thought about the talents that God has given you? Have you thought of how you can put them at the service of others? Do not bury your talents! Set your stakes on great ideals, the ideals that enlarge the heart, the ideals of service that make your talents fruitful. Life is not given to us to be jealously guarded for ourselves, but is given to us so that we may give it in turn. Dear young people, have a deep spirit! Do not be afraid to dream of great things!

Lastly, a word about the passage on the Last Judgment in which the Lord's Second Coming is described, when he will judge all human beings, the living and the dead (cf. Mt 25: 31-46). The image used by the Evangelist is that of the shepherd who separates the sheep from the goats. On his right he places those who have acted in accordance with God's will, who went to the aid of their hungry, thirsty, foreign, naked, sick or imprisoned neighbor—I said "foreign": I am thinking of the multitude of foreigners who are here in the Diocese of Rome: what do we do for them? While on his left are those who did not help their neighbor. This tells us that God will judge us on our love, on how we have loved our brethren, especially the weakest and the neediest. Of course we must always have clearly in mind that we are justified, we are saved through grace,

Set your stakes on great ideals, the ideals that enlarge the heart, the ideals of service that make your talents fruitful.

through an act of freely given love by God who always goes before us; on our own we can do nothing. Faith is first of all a gift we have received. But in order to bear fruit, God's grace always demands our openness to him, our free and tangible response. Christ comes to bring us the mercy of a God who saves. We are asked to trust in him, to correspond to the gift of his love with a good life, made up of actions motivated by faith and love.

Dear brothers and sisters, may looking at the Last Judgment never frighten us: rather, may it impel us to live the present better. God offers us this time with mercy and patience so that we may learn every day to recognize him in the poor and in the lowly. Let us strive for goodness and be watchful in prayer and in love. May the Lord, at the end of our life and at the end of history, be able to recognize us as good and faithful servants. Many thanks!

LIVE AND WALK FOREVER WITH THE HOLY SPIRIT

FIFTH SUNDAY OF EASTER • APRIL 28, 2013

ST. PETER'S SQUARE

Before closing this celebration, I would like to entrust to Our Lady the confirmands and all of you. The Virgin Mary teaches us what it means to live in the Holy Spirit and what it means to accept the news of God in our life. She conceived Jesus by the work of the Holy Spirit, and every Christian, each one of us, is called to accept the Word of God, to accept Jesus inside of us and then to bring him to everyone. Mary invoked the Holy Spirit with the Apostles in the Upper Room: we too, every time that we come together in prayer, are sustained by the spiritual presence of the Mother of Jesus, in order to receive the gift of the Spirit and to have the strength to witness to Jesus Risen. I say this in a special way to you who have received Confirmation today: may Mary help you to be attentive to what the Lord asks of you, and to live and walk forever with the Holy Spirit!

....

By coming together in prayer, you will be sustained by the spiritual presence of Mary.

I would like to extend my affectionate greeting to all the pilgrims present from so many countries. I greet in particular the children who are preparing for Confirmation, the large group led by the Sisters of Charity, the faithful of several Polish parishes and those from Bisignano, as well as the *Katholische akademische Verbindung Capitolina.*

At this moment, a special moment, I wish to raise a prayer for the many victims caused by the tragic collapse of a factory in Bangladesh. I express my solidarity with and deepest sympathies to the families who are mourning their loved ones, and I address a strong appeal from my heart that the dignity and safety of the worker always be protected.

Now, in the light of Easter, the fruit of the Holy Spirit, we turn together to the Mother of the Lord.

ST. JOSEPH THE WORKER AND THE BEGINNING OF THE MONTH OF MARY

MAY 1, 2013

ST. PETER'S SQUARE

Dear Brothers and Sisters, good morning,

Today, May 1, we celebrate St. Joseph the Worker and begin the month traditionally dedicated to Our Lady. In our encounter this morning, I want to focus on these two figures, so important in the life of Jesus, the Church and in our lives, with two brief thoughts: the first on work, the second on the contemplation of Jesus.

1. In the Gospel of St. Matthew, in one of the moments when Jesus returns to his town, to Nazareth, and speaks

in the Synagogue, the amazement of his fellow townspeople at his wisdom is emphasized. They asked themselves the question: "Is not this the carpenter's son?" (13:55). Jesus comes into our history, he comes among us by being born of Mary by the power of God, but with the presence of St. Joseph, the legal father who cares for him and also teaches him his trade. Jesus is born and lives in a family, in the Holy Family, learning the carpenter's craft from St. Joseph in his workshop in Nazareth, sharing with him the commitment, effort, satisfaction and also the difficulties of every day.

This reminds us of the dignity and importance of work. The Book of Genesis tells us that God created man and woman entrusting them with the task of filling the earth and subduing it, which does not mean exploiting it but nurturing and protecting it, caring for it through their work (cf. Gn 1:28; 2:15). Work is part of God's loving plan, we are called to cultivate and care for all the goods of creation and in this way share in the work of creation! Work is fundamental to the dignity of a person. Work, to use a metaphor, "anoints" us with dignity, fills us with dignity, makes us similar to God, who has worked and still works, who always acts (cf. Jn 5:17); it gives one the ability to maintain oneself, one's family, to contribute to the growth of one's own nation. And here I think of the difficulties which, in various countries, today afflict the world of work and business today; I am thinking of how many, and not only young people, are unemployed, often due to a purely economic conception of society, which seeks profit selfishly, beyond the parameters of social justice.

I wish to extend an invitation to solidarity to everyone, and I would like to encourage those in public office to make every effort to give new impetus to employment; this means caring for the dignity of the person, but above all I would say do

Do not be afraid of commitment, of sacrifice, and do not view the future with fear.

not lose hope. St. Joseph also experienced moments of difficulty, but he never lost faith and was able to overcome them, in the certainty that God never abandons us. And then I would like to speak especially to you young people: be committed to your daily duties, your studies, your work, to relationships of friendship, to helping others; your future also depends on how you live these precious years of your life. Do not be afraid of commitment, of sacrifice, and do not view the future with fear. Keep your hope alive: there is always a light on the horizon.

I would like to add a word about another particular work situation that concerns me: I am referring to what we could define as "slave labor," work that enslaves. How many people worldwide are victims of this type of slavery, when the person is at the service of his or her work, while work should offer a service to people so they may have dignity. I ask my brothers and sisters in the faith and all men and women of good will for a decisive choice to combat the trafficking in persons, in which "slave labor" exists.

2. With reference to the second thought: in the silence of the daily routine, St. Joseph, together with Mary, share a single common center of attention: Jesus. They accompany and nurture the growth of the Son of God made man for us with commitment and tenderness, reflecting on everything that happened. In the Gospels, St. Luke twice emphasizes the attitude of Mary, which is also that of St. Joseph: she "kept all these things, pondering them in her heart" (2:19, 51). To listen to the Lord, we must learn to contemplate, feel his constant presence in our lives and we must stop and converse with him, give him space in prayer. Each of us, even you boys and girls, young people, so many of you here this morning, should ask yourselves: "How much space do I give to the Lord? Do I stop to talk with him?" Ever since we were children, our parents have taught us to start and end the day with a prayer, to teach us to feel that the friendship and the love of God accompanies us. Let us remember the Lord more in our daily life!

And in this month of May, I would like to recall the importance and beauty of the prayer of the Holy Rosary. Reciting the Hail Mary, we are led to contemplate the mysteries of Jesus, that is, to reflect on the key moments of his life, so that, as with Mary and St. Joseph, he is the center of our thoughts, of our attention and our actions. It would be nice if, especially in this month of May, we could pray the Holy Rosary together in the family, with friends, in the parish, or some prayer to Jesus and the Virgin Mary! Praying together is a precious moment that further strengthens family life, friendship! Let us learn to pray more in the family and as a family!

Dear brothers and sisters, let us ask St. Joseph and the Virgin Mary to teach us to be faithful to our daily tasks, to live our faith in the actions of everyday life and to give more space to the Lord in our lives, to pause to contemplate his face. Thank you.

MARY, PILGRIM OF FAITH

Sixth Sunday of Easter • May 5, 2013

St. Peter's Square

At this moment of profound communion with Christ, we also feel among us the living presence of the Virgin Mary. It is a motherly presence, a familial presence, especially for you who are part of the confraternity. Love for Our Lady is one of the characteristics of popular devotion that must be respected and well directed. For this reason, I invite you to meditate on the last chapter of the Constitution of the Second Vatican Council on the Church, *Lumen Gentium*, which speaks of Mary in the mystery of Christ and of the Church. There it says that Mary "advanced in her pilgrimage of faith" (no. 58). Dear friends, in the Year of Faith I leave you this icon of Mary the pilgrim, who follows her Son Jesus and precedes us all in the journey of faith.

Today the Eastern Churches following the Julian Calendar are celebrating Easter. I wish to send a special greeting to these brothers and sisters, uniting myself with all my heart to them in proclaiming the joyful news: Christ is Risen! Gathered in prayer around Mary, let us invoke from God the gift of the Holy Spirit, the Paraclete, that he may console and comfort all Christians, especially those celebrating Easter amid trial and suffering, and guide them on the path of reconciliation and peace.

Yesterday in Brazil Francisca de Paula de Jesus, called "Nhá Chica," was proclaimed Blessed. Her simple life was totally dedicated to God and to charity, so much so that she was called "mother of the poor." I join in the joy of the Church in Brazil for this luminous disciple of the Lord.

I greet with affection all the confraternities present, having come from many Countries. Thank you for your witness to the faith! I greet too the parish groups and the families, as well as the great parade of musical bands and associations of the *Schützen* from Germany.

A special greeting goes today to the "Meter" Association on the National Day for Child Victims of Violence. And this offers me the occasion to turn my thoughts to those who have suffered and are suffering from abuse. I would like to assure them that they are present in my prayers, but I would like to strongly declare that we must all commit ourselves with clarity and courage so that every human person, especially children, who are among the most vulnerable, be always defended and protected.

I also encourage those suffering from pulmonary hypertension and their families.

THE HOLY SPIRIT, INEXHAUSTIBLE SOURCE OF LIFE

May 8, 2013

St. Peter's Square

Dear Brothers and Sisters, good morning!

The Easter Season that we are living joyfully, guided by the Church's liturgy, is *par excellence* the season of the Holy Spirit given "without measure" (cf. Jn 3:34) by Jesus Crucified and Risen. This time of grace closes with the Feast of Pentecost, in which the Church relives the outpouring of the Spirit upon Mary and the Apostles gathered in prayer in the Upper Room.

But who is the Holy Spirit? In the Creed we profess with faith: "I believe in the Holy Spirit, the Lord and Giver of life." The first truth to which we adhere in the

Creed is that the Holy Spirit is *Kýrios*, Lord. This signifies that he is truly God just as the Father and the Son; the object, on our part, of the same act of adoration and glorification that we address to the Father and to the Son. Indeed, the Holy Spirit is the Third Person of the Most Holy Trinity; he is the great gift of Christ Risen who opens our mind and our heart to faith in Jesus as the Son sent by the Father and who leads us to friendship, to communion with God.

However, I would like to focus especially on the fact that *the Holy Spirit is the inexhaustible source of God's life in us*. Man of every time and place desires a full and beautiful life, just and good, a life that is not threatened by death, but can still mature and grow to fullness. Man is like a traveler who, crossing the deserts of life, thirsts for the living water: gushing and fresh, capable of quenching his deep desire for light, love, beauty and peace. We all feel this desire! And Jesus gives us this living water: he is the Holy Spirit, who proceeds from the Father and whom Jesus pours out into our hearts. "I came that they may have life, and have it abundantly," Jesus tells us (Jn 10:10).

Jesus promised the Samaritan woman that he will give a superabundance of "living water" forever to all those who recognize him as the Son sent by the Father to save us (cf. Jn 4:5-26; 3:17). Jesus came to give us this "living water," who is the Holy Spirit, that our life might be guided by God, might be moved by God, nourished by

God. When we say that a Christian is a spiritual being we mean just this: the Christian is a person who thinks and acts in accordance with God, in accordance with the Holy Spirit. But I ask myself: and do we, do we think in accordance with God? Do we act in accordance with God? Or do we let ourselves be guided by the many other things that certainly do not come from God? Each one of us needs to respond to this in the depths of his or her own heart.

At this point we may ask ourselves: Why can this water quench our thirst deep down? We know that water is essential to life; without water we die; it quenches, washes, makes the earth fertile. In the Letter to the Romans we find these words: "God's love has been poured into our hearts through the Holy Spirit who has been given to us" (5:5). The "living water," the Holy Spirit, the Gift of the Risen One who dwells in us, purifies us, illuminates us, renews us, transforms us because he makes us participants in the very life of God that is Love. That is why, the Apostle Paul says that the Christian's life is moved by the Holy Spirit and by his fruit, which is "love, joy, peace, patience, kindness, goodness, faithfulness, gentleness, self-control" (Gal 5:22-23). *The Holy Spirit introduces us to divine life as "children in the Only Begotten Son."*

In another passage from the Letter to the Romans, that we have recalled several times, St. Paul sums it up with these words: "For all who are led by the Spirit of God are sons of God. For you . . . have received the spirit of sonship. When we cry, 'Abba! Father!' it is the Spirit himself bearing witness with our spirit that we are children of God, and if children, then heirs, heirs of God and fellow heirs with Christ, provided we suffer with him in order that we may also be glorified with him" (8:14-17). This is the precious gift that the Holy Spirit brings to our hearts: the very life of God, the life of true children, a relationship of confidence, freedom and trust in the love and mercy of God. It

What does the Holy Spirit tell us? He says: God loves you, God likes you.

also gives us a new perception of others, close and far, seen always as brothers and sisters in Jesus to be respected and loved.

The Holy Spirit teaches us to see with the eyes of Christ, to live life as Christ lived, to understand life as Christ understood it. That is why the living water, who is the Holy Spirit, quenches our life, why he tells us that we are loved by God as children, that we can love God as his children and that by his grace we can live as children of God, like Jesus. And we, do we listen to the Holy Spirit? What does the Holy Spirit tell us? He says: God loves you. He tells us this. God loves you, God likes you. Do we truly love God and others, as Jesus does? Let us allow ourselves to be guided by the Holy Spirit, let us allow him to speak to our heart and say this to us: God is love, God is waiting for us, God is Father, he loves us as a true father loves, he loves us truly and only the Holy Spirit can tell us this in our hearts. Let us hear the Holy Spirit, let us listen to the Holy Spirit and may we move forward on this path of love, mercy and forgiveness. Thank you.

WE TRUST IN THE CLOSENESS OF GOD WHO NEVER ABANDONS US

Seventh Sunday of Easter • May 12, 2013

St. Peter's Square

Dear Brothers and Sisters,

At the end of this celebration I would like to greet all of you who have come to pay homage to the new saints and in particular the official delegations from Italy, Colombia and Mexico.

May the martyrs of Otranto help the beloved Italian people to look with hope to the future, trusting in the closeness of God who never abandons us, even in difficult moments.

Through the intercession of Mother Laura Montoya may the Lord grant the Church a new missionary and evangelizing impetus and, inspired by this new saint's example of harmony and reconciliation may the beloved sons and daughters of Colombia continue to work for peace and for the just development of their homeland.

....

Look with hope to the future, trusting in the closeness of God who never abandons us.

Let us place in the hands of St. Guadalupe García Zavala all the poor, the sick and those who care for them. Let us also commend to her intercession the noble Mexican nation so that all violence and insecurity may be eradicated and that it may continue to advance on the path of solidarity and brotherly coexistence.

I am now glad to recall the beatification, yesterday, in Rome, of the priest Luigi Novarese, Founder of the International Confederation of the Volunteers of Suffering Centers and of the Silent Workers of the Cross. I join in the thanksgiving for this exemplary priest, who was able to renew the pastoral care of the sick by giving them an active role in the Church.

I greet the participants in the March for Life which took place this morning in Rome. I ask everyone to continue to pay special attention to this most important issue of respect for human life from the moment of conception. In this regard I would also like to remember the collection of signatures being made today in Italian parishes in support of the European project "One of Us." The initiative aims to guarantee embryos legal protection, safeguarding every human being from the very first moment of his or her existence. *Evangelium Vitae* Day will be a special event for those who have at heart the defense of the sacred nature of human life. It will be held here in the Vatican, in the context of the Year of Faith, next June 15 and 16.

I greet with affection all the parish groups, families, schools and young people present. Let us now turn with filial love to the Virgin Mary, Mother and Model of all Christians.

THE SPIRIT OF TRUTH

MAY 15, 2013

ST. PETER'S SQUARE

Dear Brothers and Sisters, good morning!

Today I would like to reflect on the Holy Spirit's action in guiding the Church and each one of us to the Truth. Jesus himself told his disciples: the Holy Spirit "will guide you into all the truth" (Jn 16:13), since he himself is "the Spirit of Truth" (cf. Jn 14:17; 15:26; 16:13).

We are living in an age in which people are rather skeptical of truth. Benedict XVI has frequently spoken of relativism, that is, of the tendency to consider nothing definitive and to think that truth comes from consensus or from something we like. The question arises: Does "the" truth really exist? What is "the" truth? Can we know it? Can we find it? Here springs to my mind the question of Pontius Pilate, the Roman Procurator, when Jesus reveals to him the deep meaning of his mission: "What is truth?" (Jn 18:37, 38). Pilate cannot understand that "the" Truth is standing in front of him, he cannot see in Jesus the face of the truth that is the face of God. And yet Jesus is exactly this: the Truth that, in the fullness of time, "became flesh" (cf. Jn 1:1, 14), and came to dwell among us so that we might know it. The truth is not grasped as a thing, the truth is encountered. It is not a possession, it is an encounter with a Person.

But who can enable us to recognize that Jesus is "the" Word of truth, the Only-Begotten Son of God the Father? St. Paul teaches that "no one can say 'Jesus is Lord' except by the Holy Spirit" (1 Cor 12:3). It is the Holy Spirit himself, the gift of the Risen Christ, who makes us recognize the Truth. Jesus describes him as the "Paraclete," namely, "the one who comes to our aid," who is beside us to sustain us on this journey of knowledge; and, at the Last Supper, Jesus assures the disciples that the Holy Spirit will teach them all things and remind them of all he has said to them (cf. Jn 14:26).

So how does the Holy Spirit act in our life and in the life of the Church in order to guide us to the truth? First of all he recalls and impresses in the heart of believers the words Jesus spoke and, through these very words, the law of God—as the Prophets of the Old Testament had foretold—is engraved in our heart and becomes within us a criterion for evaluation in decisions and for guidance in our daily actions; it becomes a principle to live by. Ezekiel's great prophecy is brought about: "You shall be clean from all your uncleannesses, and from all your idols I will cleanse you. A new heart I will give you, and a new spirit I will put within you. . . . And I will put my spirit within you, and cause you to walk in my statutes and be careful to observe my ordinances" (36:25-27). Indeed, it is in our inmost depths that our actions come into being: it is the heart itself that must be converted to God and the Holy Spirit transforms it when we open ourselves to him.

Then, as Jesus promised, the Holy Spirit guides us "into all the truth" (Jn 16:13); not only does he guide us to the encounter with Jesus, the fullness of the Truth, but he also guides us "into" the Truth, that is, he makes us enter into an ever deeper communion with Jesus, giving us knowledge of all the things of God. And we cannot achieve this by our own efforts. Unless God enlightens us from within, our Christian existence will be superficial. The Church's Tradition asserts that the Spirit of truth acts in our heart, inspiring that "sense of the faith" (*sensus fidei*) through which, as the Second Vatican Council states, the People of God, under the guidance of the Magisterium, adheres unfailingly to the faith transmitted, penetrates it more deeply with the right judgment, and applies it more fully in life (cf. Dogmatic Constitution *Lumen Gentium*, no. 12). Let us try asking ourselves: Am I open to the action of the Holy Spirit? Do I pray him to give me illumination, to make me more sensitive to God's things?

This is a prayer we must pray every day: "Holy Spirit, make my heart open to the word of God, make my heart open to goodness, make my heart open to the beauty of God every day." I would like to ask everyone a question: How many of you pray every day to the Holy Spirit? There will not be many but we must fulfill Jesus' wish and pray every day to the Holy Spirit that he open our heart to Jesus.

Let us think of Mary who "kept all these things, pondering them in her heart" (Lk 2:19, 51). Acceptance of the words and truth of faith so that they may become life is brought about and increases under the action of the Holy Spirit. In this regard we must learn from Mary, we must relive her "yes," her unreserved readiness to receive the Son of God in her life, which was transformed from that moment. Through the Holy Spirit, the Father

....

It is the heart itself that must be converted.

and the Son take up their abode with us: we live in God and of God. Yet is our life truly inspired by God? How many things do I put before God?

Dear brothers and sisters, we need to let ourselves be bathed in the light of the Holy Spirit so that he may lead us into the Truth of God, who is the one Lord of our life. In this Year of Faith let us ask ourselves whether we really have taken some steps to know Christ and the truth of faith better by reading and meditating on Sacred Scripture, by studying the *Catechism* and by receiving the sacraments regularly. However, let us ask ourselves at the same time what steps we are taking to ensure that faith governs the whole of our existence. We are not Christian "part-time," only at certain moments, in certain circumstances, in certain decisions; no one can be Christian in this way, we are Christian all the time! Totally! May Christ's truth, which the Holy Spirit teaches us and gives to us, always and totally affect our daily life. Let us call on him more often so that he may guide us on the path of disciples of Christ. Let us call on him every day. I am making this suggestion to you: let us invoke the Holy Spirit every day; in this way the Holy Spirit will bring us close to Jesus Christ.

WE HAVE EXPERIENCED THE BEAUTY OF UNITY

SOLEMNITY OF PENTECOST • MAY 19, 2013

ST. PETER'S SQUARE

Dear Brothers and Sisters,

This celebration of faith is drawing to a close. It began yesterday with the Vigil and culminated this morning with the Eucharist. It was a renewed Pentecost that transformed St. Peter's Square into an Upper Room beneath the open sky. We have relived the experience of the nascent Church, harmonized in prayer with Mary, the Mother of Jesus (cf. Acts 1:14). In the variety of charisms we too have experienced the beauty of unity, of being one. Moreover this is an action of the Holy Spirit who creates unity in the Church ever anew.

I would like to thank all the movements, associations, communities and ecclesial groups. You are a gift and a treasure in the Church! This is what you are! I thank in particular all of you who have come from Rome and from so many parts of the world. Always convey the power of the Gospel! Do not be afraid! Always feel joy and enthusiasm for communion in the Church! May the Risen Lord be with you constantly and may Our Lady protect you!

....

Always convey the power of the Gospel! Do not be afraid!

Let us remember in our prayers the populations of Emilia Romagna hit by the earthquake on May 20 last year. I also pray for the Federazione Italiana delle Associazioni di Volontariato in Oncologia [Italian Federation of Volunteer Associations in Oncology].

Brothers and sisters, thank you so much for your love for the Church! Have a good Sunday, a good feast day and a good lunch!